CONTROL:
Adventures at Prosperity Patch

by Kim D. H. Butler
and Spencer Shaw

CONTROL: Adventures at Prosperity Patch
Copyright © 2025 Kim D. H. Butler and Spencer Shaw

Prosperity Economics Movement
22790 Highway 259 South
Mount Enterprise, TX 75681
www.ProsperityEconomics.org

First Edition
ISBN: 979-8-9940994-3-8 (paperback)

Produced in the United States of America

Published with the assistance of Social Motion Publishing, which
specializes in books that benefit causes and nonprofits. For more
information, go to SocialMotionPublishing.com.

Acknowledgments

I love animals; I have had dogs, cats, chickens, pigs, sheep, goats, and dairy cows since 4th grade, and now I have Alpacas! I also love Prosperity Thinking. Now, I am excited to share these loves with children of all ages through my third love: reading! Whether you are an adult or have children, grandchildren, or great-grandchildren, reading with others (and playing games too!) is a fabulous bonding experience, and I am so grateful to the team of Spencer and family for bringing it to your table.

Enjoy, Kim Butler, Mount Enterprise, TX

I grew up hearing stories from my dad and kinfolk which shaped my world today. Sharing stories with kids is a fun way to help them think about big dreams. Huge thank you to my wife for leading our homeschooling and our kids for listening to these stories. A big thank you to Emma for helping Kim and I feel like children again.

We are so grateful to everyone who helps us make this book, like Amanda who leads this project and our awesome designers Cy and Holly.

Spencer Shaw

One hot summer day at Prosperity Patch, Emma, the wise Great Dane, noticed the farm's plants looking sad during the dry spells.

She gathered all her friends to talk about a big idea.

"We need a new watering system to help our plants grow, for when it doesn't rain," Emma explained.

Excited to help, the pets decided to save money together. They put all their coins into a big piggy bank to buy the new system, but they didn't have enough just yet.

A charming squirrel named Sammy, known for his slick talk and clever ideas, offered to manage their savings. "Trust me, I'll make your savings grow," Sammy promised with a sly grin.

The pets, thrilled by the idea of their money growing, agreed without asking many questions.

At first, everything seemed perfect. Sammy reported that their money was growing because of his smart choices.

They were all happy and even started dreaming about other cool things they could buy for the farm.

"Can we see how you're managing our savings?" Peanut asked one day.

Sammy hesitated and made excuses, which made Peanut suspicious. She whispered her worries to Emma.

Emma, concerned, insisted on seeing the accounts.

After a bit of a fuss, they discovered that Sammy had been using some of their money for his own little projects. Not all their savings were being tracked wisely.

Shocked and upset, the pets realized how important it was to keep an eye on their own money. They kindly but firmly asked Sammy to step aside. "We need to manage our money ourselves," Emma declared.

Miguel, the strong and dependable bull, took over managing the savings, with Zippy and Peanut helping.

They kept clear records and shared everything openly with each other.

With everyone working together and watching over their funds, their savings started to grow for real this time.

Eventually, they had enough to buy the new watering system which would help the plants continue to thrive even in very dry weather.

Their plants thrived, and they learned a valuable lesson about taking care of their own money.

As they gathered under the shade of the big oak tree, Emma shared her thoughts.

"We learned that to really take care of our money, we need to understand where it's going and make our own decisions," she said thoughtfully.

Emma's Advice:

Hey there, young saver! Here's a fun way to keep track of your money: you can start by using a special jar or a piggy bank to keep your coins and bills safe. Every time you get some money, put it in your jar.

You can even make a simple chart with your family's help, to show how much money you have. Each week, count your money and update your chart to see how it grows. Remember, saving money can help you buy something special or even help others. Keep up the great work!

Emma's Questions:

1. What kind of jar or box could you use to keep your coins and bills safe at home?
2. How do you feel when you decide to save some of your allowance instead of spending it right away?
3. Why is it important to track your money?
4. What fun thing would you like to save your money for, and how long do you think it will take to reach that goal?
5. Can you think of a time when you made a smart purchase with your money? How did you feel afterwards?

A note for your parents!

As our thank-you, the QR code below will give you a valuable white paper focused on Income Strategies at ProsperityEconomics.org/permission.